DOVER GAME AND PUZZLE

Spot-the-Difference Picture Puzzles

Compiled and Edited by
HELEN J. LEE

DOVER PUBLICATIONS, INC.
New York

Publisher's Note

THIS VOLUME CONTAINS visual puzzles specially designed to provide hours of recreation and enjoyment. Three types of puzzle are featured: Spot the Differences, Spot the Twins and Match the Shadow (each puzzle has instructions provided). To check your work (or if you are stumped), refer to the Solutions section, which begins on page 57.

Copyright

Copyright © 1996 by Singer Media Corporation.
All rights reserved under Pan American and International Copyright Conventions.

Published in Canada by General Publishing Company, Ltd., 30 Lesmill Road, Don Mills, Toronto, Ontario.
Published in the United Kingdom by Constable and Company, Ltd., 3 The Lanchesters, 162–164 Fulham Palace Road, London W6 9ER.

Bibliographical Note

Spot-the-Difference Picture Puzzles is a new work, first published by Dover Publications, Inc., in 1996, consisting of 56 puzzles and solutions from the archives of the Singer Media Corporation, San Clemente, California.

International Standard Book Number: 0-486-28908-7

Manufactured in the United States of America
Dover Publications, Inc., 31 East 2nd Street, Mineola, N.Y. 11501

SPOT THE DIFFERENCES

1. Angels

Can you spot ten differences between the two pictures?

2. Anyone for Tennis?

Can you spot ten differences between the two pictures?

3. Big Bear

Can you spot ten differences between the two pictures?

4. Picnic Lunch

Can you spot ten differences between the two pictures?

5. Haunted House

Can you spot ten differences between the two pictures?

6. Bright Globe

Can you spot ten differences between the two pictures?

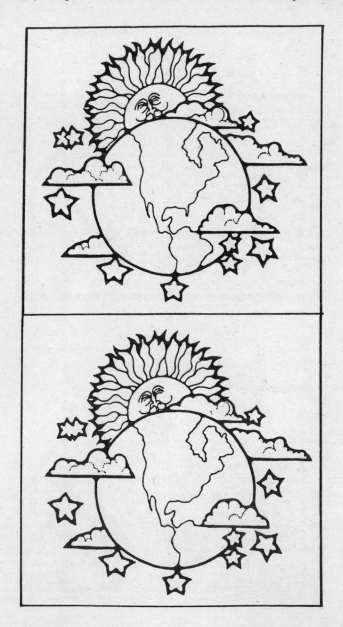

7. Harvest Time

Can you spot ten differences between the two pictures?

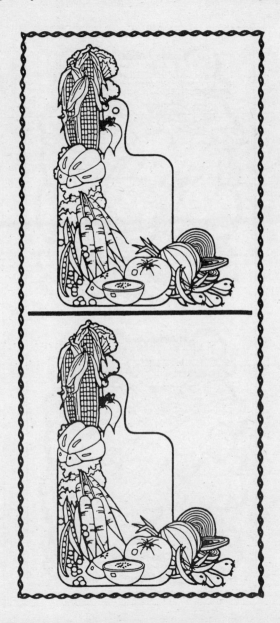

8. Tropical Fish

Can you spot ten differences between the two pictures?

9. Up, Up and Away

Can you spot ten differences between the two pictures?

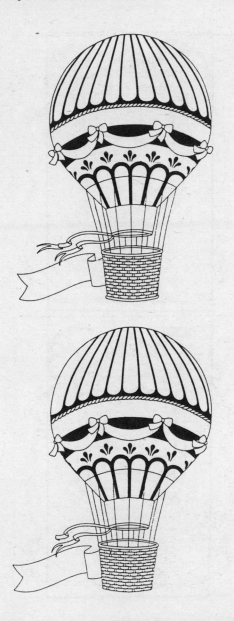

10. Ice Cream Soda

Can you spot ten differences between the two pictures?

11. Perching Cardinals

Can you spot ten differences between the two pictures?

12. New England Village

Can you spot ten differences between the two pictures?

13. Art Supplies

Can you spot ten differences between the two pictures?

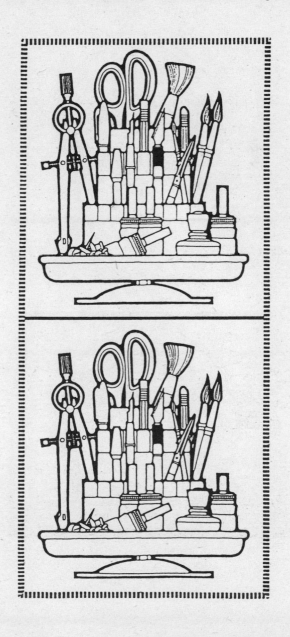

14. Golden Years

Can you spot ten differences between the two pictures?

15. Little Red Schoolhouse

Can you spot ten differences between the two pictures?

16. House Plants

Can you spot ten differences between the two pictures?

17. Victorian Kitchen

Can you spot ten differences between the two pictures?

18. Happy Home

Can you spot ten differences between the two pictures?

19. Ski Bum

Can you spot ten differences between the two pictures?

20. A Fish Tale

Can you spot ten differences between the two pictures?

SPOT THE TWINS

21.   Snowfall

Can you determine which two pictures are identical?

22. Busy Beaver

Can you determine which two pictures are identical?

23.   Constant Reader

Can you determine which two pictures are identical?

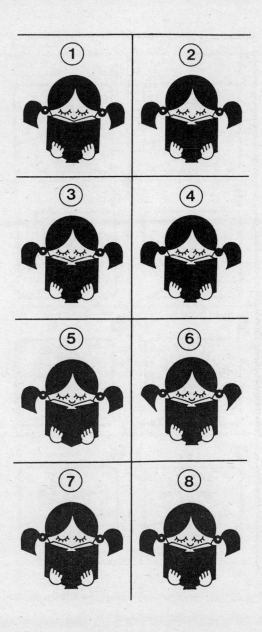

24. Arbor Day

Can you determine which two pictures are identical?

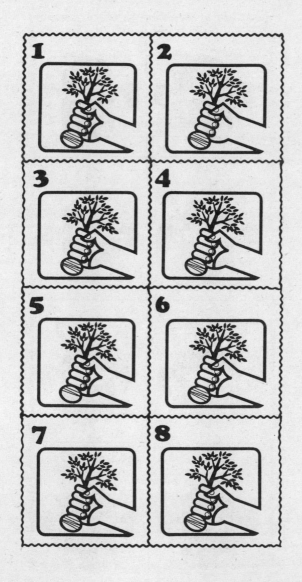

25. Sands of Time

Can you determine which two pictures are identical?

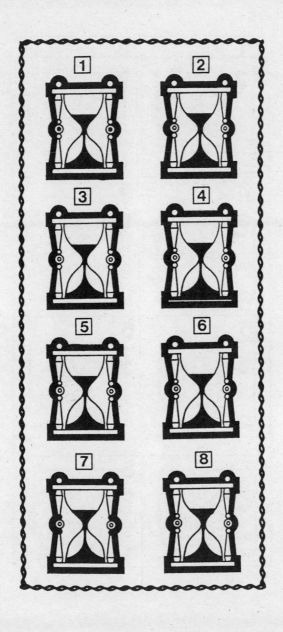

26. Ghost Story

Can you determine which two pictures are identical?

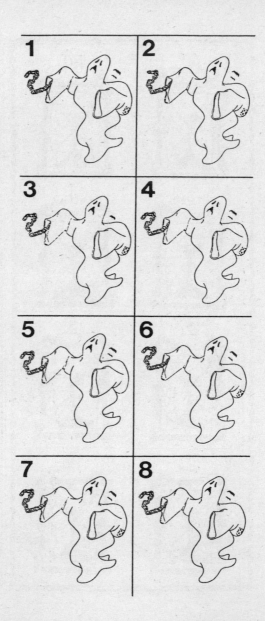

27. American Beauty

Can you determine which two pictures are identical?

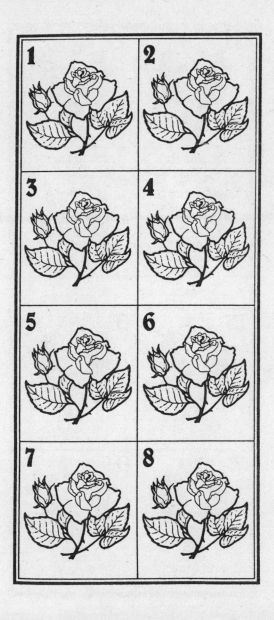

28. Frank N. Stein

Can you determine which two pictures are identical?

29. Pink Flamingoes

Can you determine which two pictures are identical?

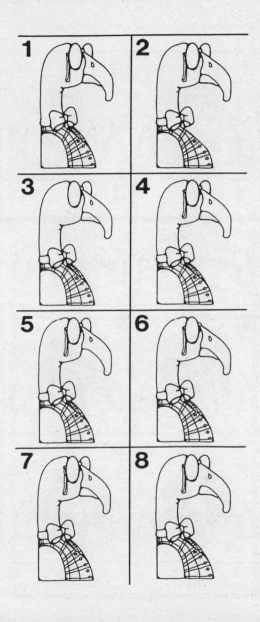

30. Lampshade

Can you determine which two pictures are identical?

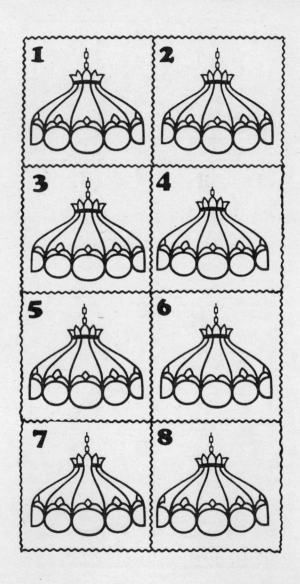

31. Happy Hour

Can you determine which two pictures are identical?

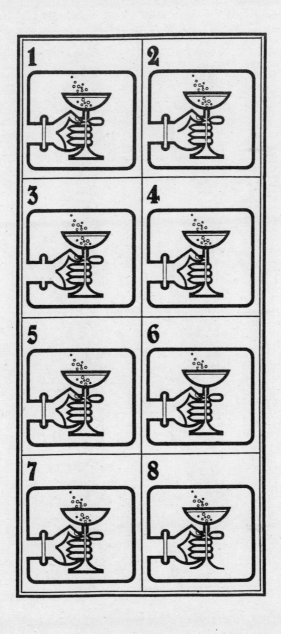

32. Snowman

Can you determine which two pictures are identical?

33. Family Car

Can you determine which two pictures are identical?

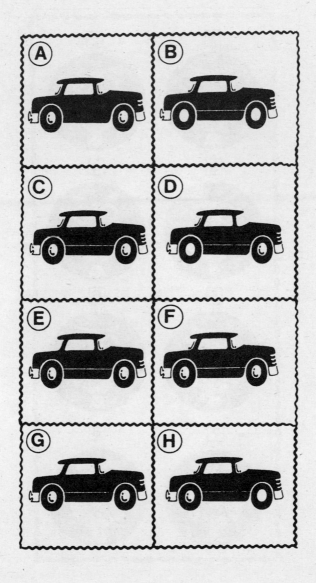

34. Wise Old Owl

Can you determine which two pictures are identical?

35. Bird with Flowers

Can you determine which two pictures are identical?

36. Dairy Farm

Can you determine which two pictures are identical?

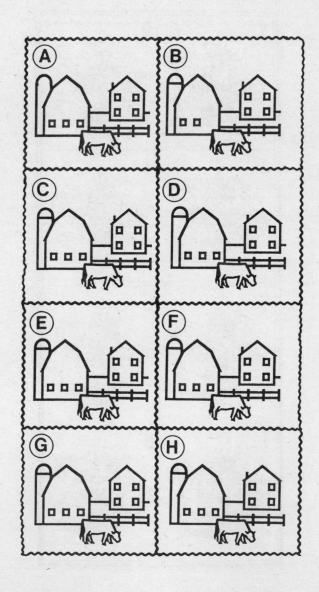

37.   Oil Lamp

Can you determine which two pictures are identical?

38.   Put the Kettle On

Can you determine which two pictures are identical?

MATCH THE SHADOW

39. The Rake's Progress

Can you determine which picture matches shadow A exactly?

40. Indian Corn

Can you determine which picture matches shadow A exactly?

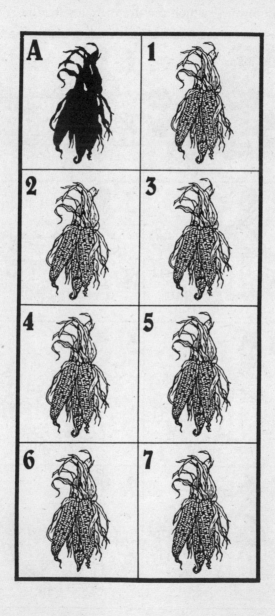

41. Dam Builder

Can you determine which picture matches shadow A exactly?

42. Ask an Owl

Can you determine which picture matches shadow A exactly?

43. Ruler of the Roost

Can you determine which picture matches shadow A exactly?

44. Saloon Keeper

Can you determine which picture matches shadow A exactly?

45. Rough Rider

Can you determine which picture matches shadow A exactly?

46. Private Transportation

Can you determine which picture matches shadow A exactly?

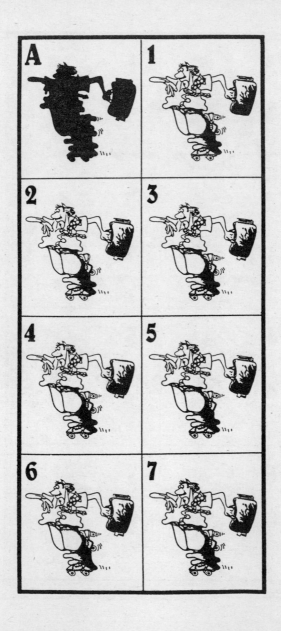

47. A Royal Pronouncement

Can you determine which picture matches shadow A exactly?

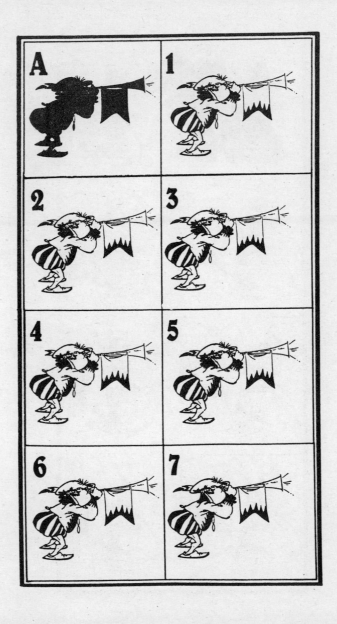

48. Dignified Dog

Can you determine which picture matches shadow A exactly?

49. Gone Fishing

Can you determine which picture matches shadow A exactly?

50. Pogo Postman

Can you determine which picture matches shadow A exactly?

51. The Devil You Say

Can you determine which picture matches shadow A exactly?

52. Thoroughly Modern Milk Cow

Can you determine which picture matches shadow A exactly?

53. Eureka!

Can you determine which picture matches shadow A exactly?

54. Rain Gear

Can you determine which picture matches shadow A exactly?

55. The Monkey's Uncle

Can you determine which picture matches shadow A exactly?

56. Robin Goodfellow

Can you determine which picture matches shadow A exactly?

SOLUTIONS

Spot the Differences

1. Angels

2. Anyone for Tennis?

4. Picnic Lunch

3. Big Bear

5. Haunted House

6. Bright Globe

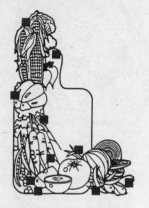

7. Harvest Time

8. Tropical Fish

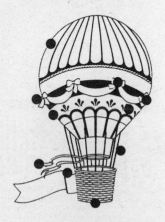

9. Up, Up and Away

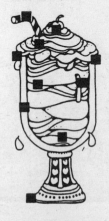

10. Ice Cream Soda

11. Perching Cardinals

12. New England Village

13. Art Supplies

14. Golden Years

15. Little Red Schoolhouse

16. House Plants

17. Victorian Kitchen

18. Happy Home

19. Ski Bum

20. A Fish Tale

Spot the Twins

21. Snowfall: 2-5

22. Busy Beaver: 2-5

23. Constant Reader: 3-8

24. Arbor Day: 4-6

25. Sands of Time: 3-8

26. Ghost Story: 4-7

27. American Beauty: 4-7

28. Frank N. Stein: 3-6

29. Pink Flamingoes: 4-7

30. Lampshade: 2-5

31. Happy Hour: 1-5

32. Snowman: 3-8

33. Family Car: C-F

34. Wise Old Owl: 4-7

35. Bird with Flowers: 2-6

36. Dairy Farm: D-E

37. Oil Lamp: 2-5

38. Put the Kettle On: 2-5

Match the Shadow

39. The Rake's Progress: A-6

40. Indian Corn: A-5

41. Dam Builder: A-6

42. Ask an Owl: A-7

43. Ruler of the Roost: A-6

44. Saloon Keeper: A-6

45. Rough Rider: A-6

46. Private Transportation: A-7

47. A Royal Pronouncement: A-3